LOS ANGELES
ANGELS

by Bernie Wilson

Published by ABDO Publishing Company, 8000 West 78th Street, Edina, Minnesota 55439. Copyright © 2011 by Abdo Consulting Group, Inc. International copyrights reserved in all countries. No part of this book may be reproduced in any form without written permission from the publisher. SportsZone™ is a trademark and logo of ABDO Publishing Company.

Printed in the United States of America,
North Mankato, Minnesota
112010
012011

Editor: Matt Tustison
Copy Editor: Nicholas Cafarelli
Interior Design and Production: Carol Castro
Cover Design: Christa Schneider

Photo Credits: Mark J. Terrill/AP Images, cover, 4, 36, 43 (top and middle); Paul Shane/AP Images, title; Lenny Ignelzi/AP Images, 7; Amy Sancetta/AP Images, 8; Julie Jacobson/AP Images, 11; AP Images, 12, 42 (top); File/AP Images, 15; Stf/HF/AP Images, 17; Photo by Focus On Sport/Getty Images, 18, 21, 42 (middle); Getty Images, 23; Photo by Ronald C. Modra/Sports Imagery/ Getty Images, 24, 42 (bottom); Lennox McLendon/AP Images, 27; Dave Tenenbaum/AP Images, 29, 30; Stephen Dunn/Allsport/Getty Images, 33; Photo by J.D. Cuban/Getty Images, 35; Chris Carlson/AP Images, 39, 41, 43 (bottom); Mark Avery/AP Images, 44; Jae C. Hong/AP Images, 47

Library of Congress Cataloging-in-Publication Data
Wilson, Bernie.
  Los Angeles Angels / by Bernie Wilson.
     p. cm. — (Inside MLB)
  Includes index.
  ISBN 978-1-61714-047-1
  1. Los Angeles Angels (Baseball team)—History—Juvenile literature. I. Title.
  GV875.A6W56 2011
  796.357'640979496—dc22
                              2010036566

TABLE OF CONTENTS

CHAPTER 1

WORLD CHAMPS AT LAST

A**fter** more than 40 years of waiting, the Anaheim Angels and their fans finally got to celebrate a World Series championship. On October 27, 2002, center fielder Darin Erstad caught Kenny Lofton's fly ball with two runners on and two outs in the top of the ninth inning. The catch preserved the Angels' 4–1 victory in Game 7 over the San Francisco Giants.

The final out set off a celebration worthy of Disneyland, which is located just a few miles from the Angels' home stadium. A World Series championship had finally come to the suburbs of Los Angeles.

"These fans have been waiting a long, long time for this," said third baseman Troy Glaus, the World Series' Most Valuable Player (MVP). "We're all happy to be part of the team to bring it to them."

Catcher Bengie Molina jumps into closer Troy Percival's arms as third baseman Troy Glaus, *left*, celebrates with them after the Angels won the 2002 World Series. It was the team's first world championship.

THEY WENT TO DISNEYLAND!

Two days after they won the 2002 World Series, the Angels went to Disneyland for a parade to celebrate their title. Jackie Autry, the widow of former owner Gene Autry, rode alongside Minnie Mouse. The Walt Disney Co. bought the Angels after Gene Autry died in 1998, so going to Disneyland was a natural. The Angels then took their celebration to a rally at the team's home stadium, Edison International Field.

Throughout the day, the Angels were mindful of what their fans had been through in waiting all those years for a championship. "I waited 10 years for something like this," right fielder Tim Salmon told the crowd at Disneyland. "But I know you guys have been waiting a lot longer. This is yours." Said manager Mike Scioscia, "For all the Angels fans who have been here from the beginning, and all the angels we had above, this championship is for you."

The Angels had been previously known for postseason heartache. They had always been overshadowed by their neighbors, the Los Angeles Dodgers. Now, they had finally done it. The championship came in the team's first World Series, no less.

"Somewhere, Gene Autry is smiling right now," Major League Baseball (MLB) commissioner Bud Selig said as he presented the trophy to the Angels.

Autry was known as "The Singing Cowboy." He owned the Angels from their first season in 1961 through 1997. He died in 1998 and never got to see his team become world champions.

He would have been proud of the team in its finest moment. The Angels had finished in third place in the American League (AL) West

Adam Kennedy rounds the bases after hitting one of his three home runs in the Angels' 13–5, series-clinching win over the Twins in Game 5 of the 2002 ALCS.

in 2001. They ended that season 41 games behind the Seattle Mariners. It took a bit to get going the next year. The Angels opened 6–14 in 2002. It was the worst start in team history.

They came back strong to finish 99–63. This was good enough for second place to the Oakland Athletics in the AL West. The Angels won the AL's wild-card playoff berth.

Darin Erstad hits a solo home run in the eighth inning of Game 6 of the 2002 World Series. The blast helped the Angels rally for a 6–5 win over the Giants and avoid elimination.

The Angels had never won a postseason series until they defeated the New York Yankees three games to one in the AL Division Series (ALDS). They then beat the Minnesota Twins in five games in the AL Championship Series (ALCS).

The all-California World Series between Anaheim and San Francisco was a back-and-forth affair. There were plenty of twists, turns, and scoring. It was the highest-scoring World Series ever. Neither team had more than a one-game lead at any point. The visiting Giants won the opener 4–3. The scoring then got crazy. Anaheim won 11–10 in Game 2 and 10–4 in Game 3. San Francisco prevailed 4–3 in Game 4. The Giants then rolled to a 16–4 victory in Game 5 to take a three-games-to-two Series lead.

All the Giants needed to do to capture the world title was win one more game. It looked as if that would happen in Game 6. The visiting Giants were nine outs away. They led 5–0. The Angels then staged the biggest comeback ever by a team facing World Series elimination.

During the comeback, Anaheim scored three runs in the seventh on a home run by Scott Spiezio. The Angels added three more in the eighth on a homer by Erstad and a two-run double by Glaus.

The Angels prevailed 6–5 to force a Game 7. Then, behind

rookie pitcher John Lackey's five strong innings and a three-run double by Garret Anderson in the third inning, the Angels won Game 7 for their first title.

That Angels team will always be remembered for its stars: Glaus, Lackey, Spiezio, Troy Percival, Tim Salmon, Adam Kennedy, and David Eckstein.

DAVID ECKSTEIN

David Eckstein is an example of how hard work, dedication, and a love for the game can pay off with a successful major league career.

Although he was only 5-foot-7 and about 175 pounds, Eckstein, as of 2010, had been a starting infielder in the major leagues since 2001. Eckstein made his big-league debut with the Angels on Opening Day of 2001, and he found ways to stay in the majors. Eckstein constantly had to prove himself to people who thought he was too small to play professional baseball.

Not only did Eckstein star with the Angels during the World Series season of 2002, but he was also named MVP of the 2006 World Series while with the St. Louis Cardinals. He moved on to the San Diego Padres beginning in the 2009 season.

Those players all moved to other teams or retired as the decade progressed. But the Angels' manager, Mike Scioscia, remained. He became the team's winningest manager. The 2002 World Series title was the third of his career. He was a catcher with the Dodgers when they won the World Series in 1981 and 1988.

Besides the heroics of the Angels, the 2002 World Series will also be known for the Rally Monkey. Two years earlier, two video-board operators took a clip of a monkey jumping around from the movie *Ace Ventura: Pet Detective.* They superimposed the words "RALLY MONKEY" over it. The Rally Monkey really took off in 2002.

"We love the monkey because of what it does for us. It's a good-luck charm," Lackey said. "But it's good not

Angels fan Steve Moreno walks toward an Edison International Field entrance with a "Rally Monkey" on his back before Game 1 of the 2002 World Series.

to see him because that means we're winning."

Forty-one years after making their debut—and 16 years after perhaps the most heartbreaking loss in team history—the Angels were indeed world champions.

CHAPTER 2

CITY OF ANGELS

Los Angeles, California, already had an MLB franchise in 1961 when a second team began playing in the city. The Dodgers had relocated from Brooklyn, New York, to Southern California in 1958. The move angered New Yorkers but thrilled Los Angeles baseball fans. Then, in December 1960, the expansion Los Angeles Angels were born. They represented the AL.

Gene Autry went to the AL expansion meeting in St. Louis, Missouri. He was seeking radio rights for his Golden West Broadcasting Company. But he ended up as owner and chairman of the Angels. The Angels had to quickly get ready for their first season. They needed to find a home stadium. The Dodgers played at the Los Angeles Coliseum while waiting for their new stadium to be built. So, the Angels moved into

First baseman Ted Kluszewski, known for cutting off his uniform sleeves, is shown in 1961. Kluszewski played for the Angels in the team's first season. It was his last season in the major leagues.

for the 1960 TV show *Home Run Derby*.

Autry chose Fred Haney as the general manager and soon hired Bill Rigney as the manager. Rigney had managed the New York and San Francisco Giants from 1956 to 1960. He also was a Giants infielder from 1946 to 1953. The first player the Angels drafted was pitcher Eli Grba. As with any other expansion club, the Angels had a mix of rookies and journeyman veterans.

The first regular-season game in team history was a memorable one. Playing on the road against the Baltimore Orioles on April 11, 1961, the Angels won 7–2. Grba pitched a complete game. Ted Kluszewski slugged two home runs.

Baseball seasons are long, however. The Angels were not able to maintain that kind of magic much that first season.

Wrigley Field. Wrigley Field had hosted a minor league team and was a replica of the famous ballpark that was the home of the Chicago Cubs. Los Angeles' Wrigley Field also had gained fame as the setting for the 1942 movie *Pride of the Yankees* and

Bo Belinsky, shown in 1962, pitched for the Angels from 1962 to 1964. Belinsky threw a no-hitter in 1962 in just his fourth start with the team.

They finished 70–91. Through 2010, that record still stood as the best mark of any expansion team in major league history.

The Angels moved into Chavez Ravine, now known as Dodger Stadium, for the 1962 season. Young left-hander Bo Belinsky made headlines by throwing the first no-hitter in team history. He and the Angels beat the visiting Orioles 2–0 on May 5, 1962. The flashy Belinsky was a perfect fit for Hollywood. The Angels were in contention for much of the season before finishing in third place in the AL at 86–76. It was a strong performance for a second-year club.

HELLO, HALOS

While the team is officially known as the Angels, it is also sometimes called the Halos. That is because a halo has been part of the logo since the team was introduced as the Los Angeles Angels in 1961.

Through 2010, the Angels had used eight different logos on their caps and four different names. From 1961 to 1969, there was a halo around the very top of their caps, between the logo and the button. Starting in 1970, the halo was moved onto the logo itself.

Through 2010, the team had been known as the Los Angeles Angels, the California Angels, the Anaheim Angels, and the Los Angeles Angels of Anaheim. During the team's history, the most frequent color scheme had been mostly blue with red trim, although the team went with a mostly blue scheme from 1997 to 2001 and then switched to red in 2002.

In 1964, the Angels' Dean Chance won the Cy Young Award. He finished 20–9 with a 1.65 earned-run average (ERA). The same year, the team began preparations to move to Anaheim, about 30 miles (48 km) south of Los Angeles. The next year, the Angels changed their name to the California Angels and began playing in the new Anaheim Stadium.

Anaheim Stadium became known as "The Big A." This was because of the A-frame scoreboard just beyond the center-field fence. The Big A stood 230 feet tall and had a halo. It was easily visible from several freeways that pass the stadium. When the stadium was expanded, The Big A was moved to the edge of the stadium parking lot.

The Angels of the 1960s had three winning seasons.

Dean Chance throws a pitch in 1966. Chance played for the Angels from 1961 to 1966 and had a record of 74–66 with a 2.83 ERA during that time.

This was a nice accomplishment for a young organization. Besides the 86–76 finish in 1962, the Halos, as they were also known, finished 82–80 in 1964 and 84–77 in 1967. Relief pitcher Minnie Rojas won the Fireman of the Year Award in 1967. He saved 27 games and went 12–9 with a 2.52 ERA. The Angels, however, finished the 1960s with back-to-back seasons in which they lost at least 90 games. The team would need time to find a permanent winning formula. But a very talented pitcher would keep things interesting in the 1970s even when the team was not successful.

CHAPTER 3

RYAN EXPRESS, THEN TEAM SUCCESS

As the Angels began play in the 1970s, it would be several years before they would make their first appearance in the postseason. But the acquisition of hard-throwing right-hander Nolan Ryan set the stage for one of the most remarkable stretches by a player in baseball history.

The Angels traded for Ryan and three other players from the New York Mets on December 10, 1971. The Angels sent popular shortstop Jim Fregosi to the Mets.

Ryan had trouble controlling his pitches while with the Mets. But he managed to tame his wildness with the Angels. His career took off. Ryan's fastballs were clocked as high as 100 miles per hour. As a result, he and his pitches were nicknamed "The Ryan Express." Ryan received the chance to become a full-time starter in 1972. He responded with a

Nolan Ryan gets ready to fire a pitch in the 1970s. Ryan threw four no-hitters for the Angels during that decade and led the AL in strikeouts seven times.

1975. At the time, he tied the big-league record for the most no-hitters set by Sandy Koufax of the Los Angeles Dodgers a decade earlier. Ryan would later establish the record for no-hitters with seven. He threw one with the Houston Astros in 1981 and two with the Texas Rangers in the early 1990s.

Surprisingly, Ryan never won a Cy Young Award. He did, however, pile up strikeouts. He fanned 383 batters in 1973. Through 2010, that total remained the most by any major league pitcher in a single season. He had 367 the next year.

Ryan won 21 games in 1973 and 22 in 1974. By 1975, left-hander Frank Tanana had joined Ryan in the rotation. Tanana led the AL in strikeouts with 269 and finished 16–9 in 1975. Tanana went 19–10 the next season and fanned 261 batters. He won 15 games in 1977

league-leading 329 strikeouts. The Angels went only 75–80 that season and finished in fifth place in the AL West. But California had a star player who kept fans interested every time he took the mound.

The Angels continued to finish in the bottom half of the division through 1977. But the best was yet to come for Ryan. He threw four no-hitters between May 15, 1973, and June 1,

Frank Tanana, *left*, and Nolan Ryan pose for a photo in the 1970s. The two players guided the Angels' pitching staff for several seasons.

and captured the AL ERA title at 2.54. He earned 18 victories in 1978. That year, because of an arm injury, he developed into more of a soft-throwing pitcher who fooled hitters. Tanana and Ryan were clearly the two best pitchers on the Angels' pitching staff for much of the 1970s. This led to the saying "Tanana and Ryan and two days of cryin'."

By 1978, however, the Angels were not cryin' much anymore. They finished 87–75 and in second place in the AL West. In addition to having Ryan and Tanana, the Angels featured an improved offense. Designated hitter Don Baylor was emerging as a top slugger. He had 34 homers with 99 runs batted in (RBIs). Catcher

NO-HITTERS

Nolan Ryan's run of no-hitters for the Angels in the 1970s was amazing.

In the second no-hitter, in which the Angels beat host Detroit 6–0 on July 15, 1973, the Tigers' Norm Cash jokingly came to the plate with a table leg before getting a real bat. Ryan also no-hit the host Kansas City Royals 3–0 on May 15, 1973, the visiting Minnesota Twins 4–0 on September 28, 1974, and the visiting Baltimore Orioles 1–0 on June 1, 1975.

The Angels' first "no-no" was by Bo Belinsky against the visiting Orioles on May 5, 1962. On July 3, 1970, Clyde Wright no-hit the visiting Oakland Athletics 4–0. Mike Witt threw a perfect game in a 1–0 win over the host Texas Rangers on September 30, 1984. Finally, Mark Langston and Witt combined on a no-hitter in a 1–0 win over the visiting Seattle Mariners on April 11, 1990.

Brian Downing and second baseman Bobby Grich had become key regulars who would be team mainstays for years.

The Angels added another key piece to the puzzle when they acquired seven-time AL batting champion Rod Carew from the Minnesota Twins before the 1979 season. The Angels gave up four players. The sweet-swinging first baseman helped California finish 88–74 and win the AL West in 1979. It was the Angels' first division title. Baylor was named league MVP after hitting 36 homers with 139 RBIs. He batted .296. Downing hit .326. Carew batted .318. Ryan and fellow pitcher Dave Frost each won 16 games.

In their first postseason series ever, the Angels squared off against the Baltimore Orioles in the 1979

Don Baylor bats in the 1979 ALCS. Baylor's MVP year helped the Angels earn their first playoff berth, but they lost in four games to the Orioles.

ALCS. Ryan started the series opener against Jim Palmer. Ryan allowed three runs in seven innings. But he did not factor in the decision. Host Baltimore won 6–3 in 10 innings. That game was Ryan's final Angels appearance. The Orioles would win the series three games to one.

Ryan left as a free agent after the 1979 season. He joined the Astros. Ryan would go on to pitch a record 27 big-league seasons. Ryan's departure was a blow for the Angels. But with the help of players such as Carew, Downing, and Grich, the team would bounce back in the early 1980s.

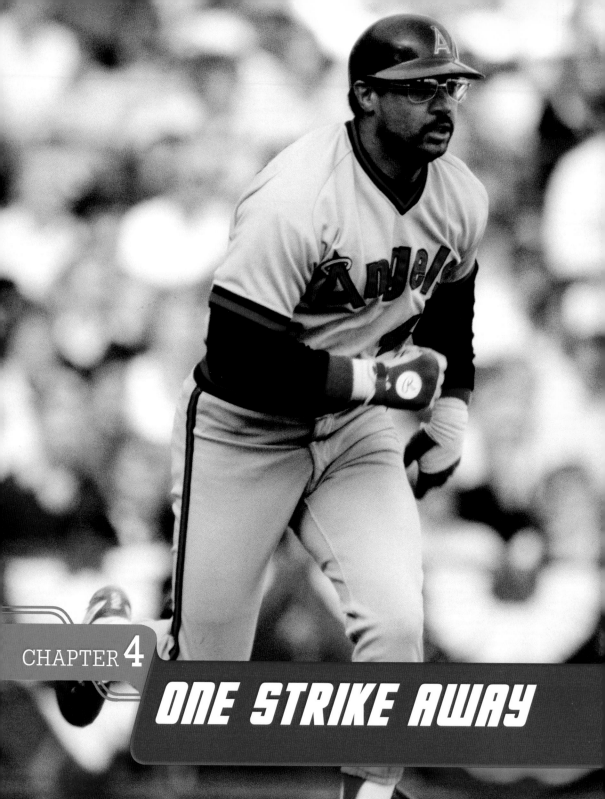

CHAPTER 4

ONE STRIKE AWAY

I n their 19th season, the Angels finally broke through and won the 1979 AL West Division title. It was an exciting season in Anaheim. The Angels led the AL in offense behind the hitting of Don Baylor, Dan Ford, and Bobby Grich.

Unfortunately for the Angels and their fans, the play-off experience was a short one. They lost in the ALCS in four games to the Baltimore Orioles. California's only win came in Game 3 in Anaheim. Larry Harlow's RBI double in the ninth inning gave California a 4–3 victory.

The Angels won the AL West and made the playoffs again in 1982. This time, star slugger Reggie Jackson was one of the team leaders. Jackson joined the club as a free agent after a five-year run with the New York Yankees. The 1982 ALCS between the Angels and the Milwaukee Brewers opened

Reggie Jackson runs after hitting the ball in the 1982 ALCS. The Angels made the playoffs in Jackson's first season with them, but they fell in five games to the Brewers.

in Anaheim. The Angels won the first two games. When the series shifted to Milwaukee, however, so did the momentum. The Brewers won the final three games of the series and headed to the World Series.

California's next trip to the playoffs came in 1986. The Angels finally were semiregular visitors to the postseason. This time, it really seemed as if they were going to make it to the World Series. California won Game 4 of the 1986 ALCS against the Boston Red Sox in thrilling fashion on Grich's 11th-inning RBI single. This gave the Angels a three-games-to-one lead. They were one win short of clinching a berth in the Fall Classic, as the World Series is known.

The next afternoon, Sunday, October 12, 1986, the Red Sox and the Angels played one of the most memorable games in major league history. Angels fans still cringe at the memory, though.

California led 5–2 in the ninth inning before visiting Boston staged an improbable comeback. Don Baylor was now playing for the Red Sox. His two-run home run trimmed Boston's deficit to 5–4. With two outs and one runner on base, California manager Gene Mauch brought in reliever

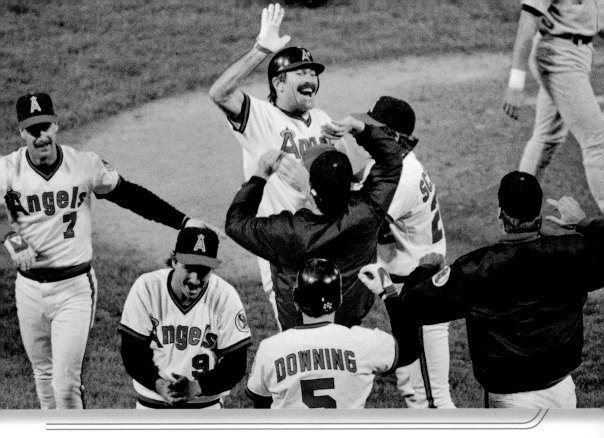

Bobby Grich, *center, with hand raised*, celebrates after his single gave the Angels a 4–3, 11-inning win in Game 4 of the 1986 ALCS.

Donnie Moore. Facing Dave Henderson, Moore was one strike away from closing it out and sending the Angels into the World Series. The champagne was on ice in the clubhouse. The fans were ready to celebrate. Instead, Henderson slammed a two-run homer to left field to lift the Red Sox into a 6–5 lead.

Carew's 3,000th Hit

Rod Carew did not start his career with the Angels, but he certainly provided a key moment in the team's history. In his final season before retiring, he reached the magical 3,000-hit plateau with a single in the third inning on August 4, 1985, at Anaheim Stadium against his former team, the Minnesota Twins. The Hall of Famer finished his career with 3,053 hits.

WALLY WORLD

Wally Joyner was a rookie first baseman with the Angels in 1986. He immediately became a fan favorite with his bat and his glove. He replaced Rod Carew, who had retired after the previous season.

Joyner became so popular that fans began calling Anaheim Stadium "Wally World," a reference to Disneyland and a fictitious theme park in *National Lampoon's Vacation*. Joyner hit .290 with 22 home runs and 100 RBIs. He made the AL All-Star team and was second in the league's Rookie of the Year voting.

Joyner fared even better in 1987, when he set career highs with 34 home runs and 117 RBIs and batted .285.

Joyner left as a free agent after the 1991 season but returned to play with the Angels in 2001.

The Angels tied the score in the bottom of the ninth inning and had the bases loaded with one out but could not push across the winning run. The game went into extra innings. The Red Sox won 7–6 in 11 innings on Henderson's sacrifice fly that brought in Baylor.

The Angels and their fans were shocked. Anaheim Stadium was hushed, except for the sound of the Red Sox celebrating. The series was not over. But it might as well have been. After being one strike away from going to the World Series, the Angels had to travel back to Boston for Games 6 and 7 at Fenway Park. Their spirits crushed, the Angels lost both games. The scores were 10–4 and 8–1. They watched the Red Sox claim the pennant that they had all but wrapped up back in Anaheim.

Manager Gene Mauch, *right*, and designated hitter Reggie Jackson watch from the dugout during the Angels' 10–4 loss in Game 6 of the 1986 ALCS. California would lose the series in seven games.

It would be 16 long seasons before the Angels would make their way back to the playoffs.

Sutton's 300th Win

In Southern California, Don Sutton is usually best remembered as having pitched for the Los Angeles Dodgers from 1966 to 1980. However, like Rod Carew and Reggie Jackson, he achieved a career milestone while with the Angels. On June 18, 1986, he earned the 300th victory of his career, beating the Texas Rangers 5–1 at Anaheim Stadium.

CHAPTER 5

UNDER THE RADAR

The Angels' sudden exit from the playoffs in 1986 seemed to set the tone for the next 13 years. The team struggled for the most part from 1987 until Mike Scioscia was hired as manager before the 2000 season. Still, it was a time when several recognizable players either began their careers or joined the Halos.

The Angels tumbled to identical records of 75–87 in 1987 and 1988. Gene Mauch's last season as manager was in 1987. He had managed the team since 1981. Cookie Rojas began the 1988 campaign as manager before Moose Stubing replaced him late in the season.

Amidst the team's struggles, Jim Abbott provided the Angels and their fans with inspiration. Abbott was born without a right hand. But he became a star pitcher. He had a successful college career at the University of Michigan. He then helped the United States

Rookie Jim Abbott pitches during the 1989 season. Abbott, who was born without a right hand, won 10 games or more in three different seasons for the Angels.

TRAGEDIES

The Angels have been affected by tragedies over the years.

Outfielder Lyman Bostock was shot and killed on September 23, 1978, while visiting his hometown of Gary, Indiana, after a game in Chicago against the White Sox.

On July 18, 1989, Donnie Moore committed suicide in his Southern California home. He was still haunted by that pitch against the Red Sox in the 1986 ALCS, as well as injuries that kept him from catching on with another team.

On April 9, 2009, just hours after making a strong season debut with his father watching from the stands, rookie pitcher Nick Adenhart and two others were killed by a drunk driver not far from Angel Stadium. Adenhart was only 22. The Angels delayed their game the next night. When they returned to action, they honored Adenhart by painting his No. 34 in red on the back of the mound at Anaheim Stadium.

win the gold medal at the 1988 Olympics. He was selected by the Angels in the first round of the 1988 amateur draft but did not begin his professional career until spring training in 1989.

Abbott was so good that he did not spend a single day in the minor leagues before joining the Angels. He had a record of 12–12 with a 3.92 ERA in 1989 as a rookie.

Abbott used ingenuity to overcome his disability. As he delivered a pitch with his left hand, he held a glove against his chest with his right arm. While completing his follow through, he would quickly switch the glove to his left hand so he could handle balls that might be hit back to him. Abbott was traded to the New York Yankees after the 1992 season. He pitched a no-hitter for the Yankees in 1993.

Chuck Finley lets go of a pitch in 1989. Finley finished 16–9 that year. The 6-foot-6 left-hander won a team-record 165 games with the Angels.

He was reacquired by the Angels in July 1995 and remained with them through 1996.

The Angels had a 91–71 record in 1989. This was good enough for third place in the AL West. That would be their best record until their World Series season of 2002, when they went 99–63.

Still, the down years were a time when players such as

Tim Salmon, J. T. Snow, Mark Langston, and Chuck Finley became Angels mainstays. Salmon won the AL Rookie of the Year Award in 1993 after hitting 31 home runs and driving in 95 runs. Snow, one of three players obtained from the Yankees for Abbott, was a standout defensive first baseman. He could also hit for power.

Langston and Finley anchored the pitching staff for much of the 1990s. They each had 15 wins in 1995. That year, the Angels led the AL West for much of the season. The Seattle Mariners jumped into the race late in the season. The teams finished the strike-shortened season tied with 78–66 records. This forced a one-game playoff. Seattle hosted the game in the noisy Kingdome. AL Cy Young Award winner Randy Johnson was too much for the Halos, who lost 9–1.

The Angels did not come close to making the playoffs again the rest of the decade. There were major changes off the field, however. The Los Angeles Rams of the National Football League (NFL) moved to St. Louis, Missouri, after the 1994 season. This allowed the Angels to turn Anaheim Stadium into a cozy, baseball-only

Right fielder Tim Salmon is shown in 1995, when he had 34 home runs and 105 RBIs. Salmon played his entire 14-season career with the Angels.

stadium. The Walt Disney Co. purchased part of the team from Gene Autry, who died in 1998. After stumbling to last place in 1999, the Angels were ready for a fresh start under Scioscia.

"Mr. Angel"

Right fielder Tim Salmon earned the nickname "Mr. Angel" in his 14 seasons with the team. He was the AL Rookie of the Year in 1993, and he went on to become the team's all-time leader in a handful of categories before he retired after the 2006 season. Through 2010, his 299 homers were an Angels record. He also hit two home runs in Game 2 of the 2002 World Series.

CHAPTER 6

THE SCIOSCIA ERA

Since becoming manager before the 2000 season, Mike Scioscia has guided the Angels through the most successful period in team history. It is perhaps no surprise, considering that Scioscia was successful as a player with the Los Angeles Dodgers.

Scioscia was manager of the Dodgers' Triple-A team in Albuquerque, New Mexico, when the Angels hired him in November 1999. The team was coming off a disappointing season that led to the resignations of manager Terry Collins and general manager Bill Bavasi.

The Angels had been picked by many baseball followers to win the AL West but instead finished in last place at 70–92. New general manager Bill Stoneman selected Scioscia as manager.

It was a wise choice. Through 2010, the Angels had

Mike Scioscia speaks at a news conference on November 18, 1999. The former big-league catcher had just been named the Angels' manager.

times in 39 seasons and had failed to reach the World Series.

Scioscia was named the AL Manager of the Year in 2002 and 2009. He also led the Angels to the best record in club history, 100–62 in 2008.

Scioscia took a talented lineup and shaped it into a team that finished 82–80 in his first year. Among the stars on his team were Garret Anderson, Troy Glaus, Darin Erstad, and Tim Salmon. The Angels dropped to 75–87 in 2001. But they rebounded to go 99–63 and win the World Series the next season.

The Angels added another star in 2004 when they signed former Montreal Expos outfielder Vladimir Guerrero as a free agent. It was a great move, considering that Guerrero was voted the AL MVP that season. He hit .337 with 39 home runs and scored a league-high

made it to the playoffs six times under Scioscia and won their first World Series. The Angels had captured five AL West Division crowns under Scioscia. In the year that they won the World Series, 2002, they made the playoffs as the AL's wild-card team. Before Scioscia's arrival, the Angels had qualified for the playoffs only three

Vladimir Guerrero, *left*, greets Garret Anderson after Anderson homered in 2004. The Angels won 92 games that year. It was one of six seasons in the 2000s in which the team reached 90 victories.

124 runs. The Angels won the AL West at 92–70. Their stay in the playoffs was short, however. The Boston Red Sox, who went on to win the World Series, swept the Angels in three games.

Scioscia has managed some of the best players in Angels history. Among them are right fielder Guerrero, right-hander Bartolo Colon (the 2005 AL Cy Young Award winner), center fielder Erstad, third baseman Glaus, right-handed relief pitcher Troy Percival, center fielder Torii Hunter, and left fielder Anderson.

Through 2010, the Angels had not made it back to the World Series since that magical season of 2002. But they had become regular participants in the postseason under Scioscia and owner Arte Moreno. Moreno bought the team in 2003.

In 2009, the Angels overcame the tragic loss of rookie pitcher Nick Adenhart in a car crash and swept the Red Sox in three games in the ALDS. The Angels fell in six games to the New York Yankees in the ALCS. The 2009 postseason marked the first time they had won a playoff series since 2005. That year, they beat the Yankees in the opening round before losing to the Chicago White Sox in the ALCS.

The Angels finished 80–82 in 2010 and did not make the playoffs. Pitcher Ervin Santana was one of the team's top players again. He finished 17–10. It marked the third time in five years that he reached 16 wins. Fellow right-hander Jered Weaver went 13–12 with a 3.01 ERA and an AL-high 233 strikeouts. Weaver reached the 10-win mark for the fifth time in his five big-league seasons, all with the Angels. Four players hit 20 or more home runs for Los Angeles. Mike Napoli had 26, Hunter added 23, newcomer

Arte Moreno

Arte Moreno became the first Hispanic American to own a big-league baseball team when he purchased the Angels from The Walt Disney Co. in May 2003. He made a fortune in outdoor advertising and has been equally successful with the Angels. He immediately became popular with the fans when he cut ticket prices. The Angels are known as one of the most fan-friendly teams in all of professional sports. Moreno had previous baseball experience as part of a group that owned a minor league team in Salt Lake City, Utah, in the mid-1980s.

On April 10, 2009, Angels pitcher Jered Weaver pays tribute to former teammate Nick Adenhart at a banner at Angel Stadium. Adenhart was killed the day before by a drunk driver.

Hideki Matsui contributed 21, and Bobby Abreu pitched in with 20. The team batted only .248, however, and had trouble generating runs.

The Angels were disappointed in their 2010 season. But based on the success they had enjoyed under Scioscia, they were confident they would be competing in the playoffs again sometime soon.

TIMELINE

1960 On December 6, an AL expansion team, the Los Angeles Angels, is awarded to Gene Autry, a movie, radio, and television performer known as "The Singing Cowboy."

1961 On April 11, the Angels defeat the host Baltimore Orioles 7–2 in the first regular-season game in team history.

1973 Nolan Ryan throws his first no-hitter, winning 3–0 over the host Kansas City Royals on May 15. On July 15, he throws his second no-hitter as the visiting Angels defeat the Detroit Tigers 6–0.

1974 On September 28, Ryan hurls his third no-hitter as the Angels beat the visiting Minnesota Twins 4–0.

1975 Ryan pitches no-hitter number four, lifting the Angels to a 1–0 home victory over the Orioles.

1979 The Angels finish 88–74 and capture their first division title. In their first postseason appearance, the Angels lose three games to one to Baltimore in the ALCS.

1982 California goes 93–69 to win its second AL West crown. The Angels lose again in the ALCS, however, falling three games to two to the Brewers. Milwaukee wins the series' final three games.

1986 California finishes 90–72 to win the AL West by five games. The Angels take a three-games-to-one lead in the ALCS over the Boston Red Sox. But Boston rallies late in Game 5 and wins 7–6 in 11 innings. The Red Sox win Games 6 and 7 in Boston, as well, leaving the Angels heartbroken.

1996	The Walt Disney Co. takes 25 percent ownership and immediate control of daily operations of the Angels on May 15.
1999	Mike Scioscia, a former standout catcher with the Los Angeles Dodgers, is hired as the Angels' manager on November 18.
2002	The Angels finish 99–63 and capture the AL's wild-card playoff berth. Anaheim defeats the New York Yankees three games to one in the ALDS and the Twins four games to one in the ALCS. The Angels win the final two games of the World Series at home to defeat the San Francisco Giants for their first Series title. Anaheim third baseman Troy Glaus is named Series MVP.
2003	Arte Moreno is introduced as owner of the Angels on May 22.
2005	The Angels win their second consecutive AL West title, going 95–67. However, the team, which became known as the Los Angeles Angels of Anaheim this season, loses for a second straight year in the postseason without reaching the World Series.
2009	The Angels go 97–65 and claim their third straight AL West championship. This gives them five division titles in Scioscia's first 10 seasons as manager. They again come up short of qualifying for the World Series, though, losing four games to two to the Yankees in the ALCS.

QUICK STATS

FRANCHISE HISTORY

Los Angeles Angels (1961–64)
California Angels (1965–96)
Anaheim Angels (1997–2004)
Los Angeles Angels of Anaheim
    (2005–)

WORLD SERIES
(wins in bold)

2002

AL CHAMPIONSHIP SERIES
(1969–)

1979, 1982, 1986, 2002, 2005, 2009

KEY PLAYERS
(position[s]; seasons with team)

Don Baylor (OF/DH; 1977–82)
Rod Carew (IB; 1979–85)
Dean Chance (SP; 1961–66)

David Eckstein (IF; 2001–04)
Chuck Finley (SP; 1986–99)
Jim Fregosi (SS; 1961–71)
Troy Glaus (3B; 1998–2004)
Bobby Grich (IF; 1977–86)
Vladimir Guerrero (OF/DH;
    2004–09)
Torii Hunter (OF; 2008–)
Reggie Jackson (OF/DH; 1982–86)
Troy Percival (RP; 1995–2004)
Francisco Rodriguez (RP; 2002–08)
Nolan Ryan (SP; 1972–79)
Tim Salmon (RF/DH; 1992–2004,
    2006)

KEY MANAGERS

Gene Mauch (1981–82, 1985–87):
    379-332; 5–7 (postseason)
Mike Scioscia (2000–):
    980–802; 21–24 (postseason)

HOME PARKS

Wrigley Field-Los Angeles (1961)
Chavez Ravine (Dodger Stadium)
    (1962–65)
Angel Stadium (1966–)
    Known as Anaheim Stadium
    (1966–97)
    Known as Edison International
    Field (1998–2003)

* All statistics through 2010 season

Del Webb's construction company was awarded the contract to build Anaheim Stadium. At the time, he was co-owner of the New York Yankees, who also play in the AL. "This will be my dream stadium," Webb told the crowd during ground-breaking ceremonies on August 31, 1964. "I've tried to observe the right and wrong of every stadium in the country. We want to get all the right things in this one and leave out all the wrong things."

More than 40 years, two major renovations, and a handful of name changes later, the Angels' home ballpark is still going strong. The team renamed it Angel Stadium before the 2004 season after it had been known as Edison International Field for several years. The original Anaheim Stadium had been expanded in 1979 and 1980 to accommodate the Los Angeles Rams of the NFL. The Rams moved to St. Louis after the 1994 season, and Anaheim Stadium was renovated after the 1996 season to a beautiful baseball-only configuration. Among the nice touches are two giant Angels caps and equally large bats that decorate the main entrance. Just beyond the center-field fence is a giant rock pile with a fountain.

"Every night, I'll take a lap to talk with our fans and see what's going on." —Arte Moreno, after buying the Angels in 2003. Moreno is popular with fans because he lowered ticket and concessions prices.

The All-Star Game was played in Anaheim, California, for the third time on July 13, 2010. The NL won 3–1 for its first victory since 1996. Hall of Famer Rod Carew threw the ceremonial first pitch to Angels outfielder Torii Hunter. Former Angels star Vladimir Guerrero received a warm welcome even though he was by then a member of the AL West-rival Texas Rangers.

GLOSSARY

acquire

To receive a player through trade or by signing as a free agent.

berth

A place, spot, or position, such as in the baseball playoffs.

designated hitter

A baseball player whose only job is to hit. He does not play in the field.

draft

A system used by professional sports leagues to select new players in order to spread incoming talent among all teams.

expansion

In sports, the addition of a franchise or franchises to a league.

franchise

An entire sports organization, including the players, coaches, and staff.

free agent

A player free to sign with any team of his choosing after his contract expires.

general manager

The executive who is in charge of the team's overall operation. He or she hires and fires managers and coaches, drafts players, and signs free agents.

pennant

A flag. In baseball, it symbolizes that a team has won its league championship.

postseason

Games played in the playoffs by the top teams after the regular-season schedule has been completed.

rookie

A first-year professional athlete.

veteran

An individual with great experience in a particular endeavor.

wild card

Playoff berths given to the best remaining teams that did not win their respective divisions.

FOR MORE INFORMATION

Further Reading

Snyder, John. *Angels Journal: Year by Year and Day by Day with the Los Angeles Angels Since 1961*. Cincinnati: Clerisy Press, 2010.

Travers, Steven, and Ross Newhan. *Angels Essential: Everything You Need to Know to Be a Real Fan*. Chicago: Triumph Books, 2007.

Vecsey, George. *Baseball: A History of America's Favorite Game*. New York: Modern Library, 2008.

Web Links

To learn more about the Los Angeles Angels, visit ABDO Publishing Company online at **www.abdopublishing.com**. Web sites about the Angels are featured on our Book Links page. These links are routinely monitored and updated to provide the most current information available.

Places to Visit

Angel Stadium
2000 Gene Autry Way
Anaheim, CA 92806
714-940-2000
mlb.mlb.com/ana/ballpark/index.jsp
Angel Stadium has been home to the Angels since 1966. The team plays 81 regular-season games here each year.

Angels Spring Training
Tempe Diablo Stadium
2200 West Alameda Drive
Tempe, AZ 85282
480-350-5205
www.tempe.gov/diablo
Tempe Diablo Stadium has been the spring-training home of the Angels since 1993.

**National Baseball
Hall of Fame and Museum**
25 Main Street
Cooperstown, NY 13326
1-888-HALL-OF-FAME
www.baseballhall.org
This hall of fame and museum highlights the greatest players and moments in the history of baseball. Rod Carew, Reggie Jackson, and Nolan Ryan are among the former Angels enshrined here.

INDEX

About the Author

Bernie Wilson has worked for The Associated Press since 1984, based in Spokane, Washington; Los Angeles, California; and San Diego, California. He has written about Major League Baseball on a regular basis since 1988, beginning with the California Angels and the Los Angeles Dodgers, and has covered the San Diego Padres since 1991.